3 1628 00085 1924

P9-DHT-919

Avon Public Library
280 West Main Street
Avon, Mass. 02322

2/04

THE TRIAL OF LEOPOLD AND LOEB

A Primary Source Account

Simone Payment

rosen central
Primary Source™

The Rosen Publishing Group, Inc., New York

2|04
j345.73
P

Published in 2004 by The Rosen Publishing Group, Inc.
29 East 21st Street, New York, NY 10010

Copyright © 2004 by The Rosen Publishing Group, Inc.

First Edition

All rights reserved. No part of this book may be reproduced in any form without permission in writing from the publisher, except by a reviewer.

Manufactured in the United States of America

Unless otherwise attributed, all quotes in this book are excerpted from court transcripts.

Library of Congress Cataloging-in-Publication Data

Payment, Simone.
The Trial of Leopold and Loeb: a primary source account/by Simone Payment.
    p. cm.—(Great trials of the twentieth century)
Includes bibliographical references and index.
ISBN 0-8239-3970-7 (library binding)
1. Leopold, Nathan Freudenthal, 1904 or 5–1971—Trials, litigation, etc. 2. Loeb, Richard A., 1905 or 6–1936—Trials, litigation, etc.
3. Trials (Murder)—Illinois—Cook County.
I. Title. II. Series.
KF224.L46 P39 2004
345.73'02523—dc21

                                        2002153452

CONTENTS

In this 1924 photograph, taken during their trial for the kidnapping and murder of Bobby Franks, confessed killers Nathan Leopold and Richard Loeb laugh at a comment made in court. The carefree attitude they displayed throughout the trial reflected the personalities of the two friends, who shared an oddly intense relationship and were convinced they could commit the perfect crime.

INTRODUCTION

There had already been more than 150 murders in Chicago in 1924 by the time the body of Bobby Franks was found on May 21. People in Chicago were not surprised to hear about the crime. They were used to hearing stories about gangsters and robberies and murders. They soon learned, however, that fourteen-year-old Bobby Franks had been kidnapped and murdered by two boys not much older than Bobby. The more people learned about the case, the more shocked they became.

Within a few weeks, people in Chicago knew that Bobby Franks had been kidnapped and murdered by Nathan Leopold Jr. and Richard Loeb. The killers were both extremely intelligent and came from wealthy families. People could not understand why nineteen-year-old Leopold and eighteen-year-old Loeb had murdered their young neighbor. Leopold and Loeb themselves could not really answer that question. The young men had simply set out to commit a perfect crime and believed they would never be caught. They chose Bobby Franks for no particular reason. They just saw him walking down the street the day they decided to commit their crime.

As the weeks went by, the newspapers in Chicago printed more and more stories about the murder and about the murderers. When Leopold and Loeb confessed that they had committed the crime, newspapers printed all the details. Soon the newspapers began referring to the case as the Crime of the Century.

The case became even more interesting to Chicago residents when they learned that Clarence Darrow would be defending the two young men. Darrow was a very well-known lawyer who had successfully defended many criminals.

Darrow knew that he was taking on another difficult case. Robert Crowe was the lawyer prosecuting the case, and he was determined to get the death penalty for Leopold and Loeb. Many people in Chicago believed that Leopold and Loeb deserved to die for what they had done. Darrow had been opposed to the death penalty for many years. He felt strongly that Leopold and Loeb were too young to die. He hoped that if he won their case it would make people stop and think about the death penalty and how wrong it was. His goal was to one day get rid of the death penalty for good.

By the time Leopold and Loeb went to trial in July of 1924, everyone knew they were guilty. People looked forward to the trial anyway. They hoped to hear even more details of the case. They were eager to see Clarence Darrow in action. Most of all, they wanted to see if Leopold and Loeb would be sentenced to death.

The trial turned out to be all that Chicago residents had hoped for—and more. It was long and full of details of the lives of Leopold and Loeb. Darrow used some unexpected strategies, and he argued long and convincingly that Leopold and Loeb should not be put to death. The case of *State of Illinois v. Leopold and Loeb* is still remembered as one of the great trials of the twentieth century.

COMMITTING THE PERFECT CRIME

Late at night on Wednesday, May 21, 1924, the phone rang at the Franks house. Mrs. Franks answered the phone. She later testified that the voice on the phone told her, "Your son has been kidnapped. He is all right. There will be further news in the morning." Mrs. Franks hung up the phone and then fainted.

Her son, Bobby, had not returned from school that afternoon. It was unusual for him to be late. By dinnertime the family was very worried and had begun calling all his friends. No one knew where Bobby was. His friends said he had stayed after school to umpire a baseball game. They had last seen him walking home after the game.

Bobby's father was out searching for his son when the phone call came. When he returned home and heard about the call he was worried. He didn't know if he should call the police. If he did, the kidnappers might find out and then hurt Bobby.

The next day, the Franks family got a letter telling them that Bobby was safe. The letter told them to get $10,000 for ransom and to wait for another phone call with instructions on where to deliver the money. If they followed the instructions, Bobby would not be harmed. The Frankses would soon find out that their son was not safe after all.

A BODY IS DISCOVERED

The same day that the Frankses received the ransom letter, the body of a young boy was discovered near Wolf Lake, just outside Chicago. Some

On the day after his murder, Bobby Franks's body was discovered by rail workers, who spied a foot protruding from nearby shrubbery. On May 23, 1924, police officers brought news cameras to the site where the body was hidden, as shown in this photograph. Leopold and Loeb knew of this area outside Chicago, at the 121st Street and Pennsylvania rail tracks, because Leopold often bird-watched there.

men working on railroad tracks found the body stuffed into a ditch filled with water. There were no clothes on the boy, but there was a pair of eyeglasses near the body.

At the same time that the body was being discovered, Mr. Franks was going to the bank to get $10,000. He had also decided to tell the police about the phone call and the letter. He hurried home with the money to wait for more instructions from the kidnappers.

Meanwhile, James Mulroy, a young reporter at the *Chicago Daily News*, heard about the kidnapping of Bobby Franks. He went to the Frankses' home to see if he could find out more. Alvin Goldstein, another young reporter at the *Daily News*, heard about the discovery by the railroad tracks. Goldstein rushed to the funeral home where the body had been taken and called the *Daily News* to give them a description. His boss at the newspaper told him about the kidnapping of Bobby Franks. After more phone calls and finally a positive identification by Bobby's uncle, it was determined that the body found in the ditch was that of Bobby Franks.

Jacob Franks, the millionaire father of Bobby Franks, poses for a *Chicago Daily News* photographer in 1924, in this photograph now housed in the Chicago Historical Society. A Chicago real estate tycoon, Franks was known as "Honest Jake" for his reputation as a fair and square businessman.

THE KILLERS

The day Bobby Franks's body was discovered, the murderers went about their usual business. Nathan Leopold Jr. attended his law school classes at the University of Chicago. He met his good friend Richard Loeb for lunch. After lunch they called Mr. Franks to give him directions for where to deliver the ransom. What they didn't know was that right after they hung up with him, Mr. Franks learned that Bobby was dead. He never showed up at the drugstore where he was supposed to wait for another phone call from them.

Richard Loeb *(left)* and Nathan Leopold are photographed on the first day of their trial, July 21, 1924, in Chicago, Illinois. Years later, in his autobiography, *Life Plus Ninety-Nine Years* (1974), Leopold would write of his friend, "Dick . . . just seemed able to push an imaginary button and turn on the charm . . . But then there was that other side to him. In the crime, for instance, he didn't have a single scruple of any kind. He wasn't immoral; he was just plain amoral—unmoral, that is. Right and wrong didn't exist. He'd do anything—anything. And it was all a game to him."

When Mr. Franks did not arrive at the drugstore, Leopold and Loeb began to worry. Then they read in the newspaper that the body of a young boy had been discovered that morning. They knew it was Bobby, and they knew they were not going to get the $10,000 from Mr. Franks. Leopold and Loeb still weren't worried about being caught. They believed that they had planned so well that no one would ever figure out they were the killers.

THE PLAN

Leopold and Loeb had become friends when Leopold was fifteen and Loeb was fourteen. They were both very smart and had many things in common. Their fathers were successful businessmen, and the boys dressed well, drove nice cars, and lived in big houses. Another thing they had in common was that they thought they were better than everyone else. They thought rules did not apply to them. Leopold and Loeb did not always get along, but they made many plans to commit crimes. Loeb had read many detective stories and books about crime. He spent a lot of time thinking about how to commit crimes. Together Leopold and Loeb set fires, threw bricks through windows, and stole things. Eventually these small crimes were not enough for them. They decided to commit a much larger crime.

Leopold and Loeb had spent several months planning their crime. They had bought rope and a weapon and other things they would need. They had planned how they would get rid of the body. Leopold knew a spot where he thought no one would discover the body for many days. They thought of ways to collect the ransom money. They decided to have the money thrown from a moving train. Leopold and Loeb practiced throwing bundles from moving trains to see where they would land. They also planned how to give instructions to the victim's family.

Although Leopold and Loeb had spent a lot of time planning the crime, they had not decided who their victim would be. They considered

A PRIZE FOR THE REPORTERS

James Mulroy and Alvin Goldstein played a very important role in the Leopold and Loeb case. They helped put together the pieces of the puzzle. They followed several leads during the investigation that led to Leopold and Loeb being discovered. They wrote many stories about the case and the trial. When the case was over, they each received a reward of $1,500 for their part in the case. They also won the Pulitzer Prize, an important award for newspaper reporters.

kidnapping Loeb's younger brother, Tommy, and had even thought about kidnapping and murdering their own fathers. In the end they just decided to kidnap anyone who seemed like an easy target. When he confessed to the crime, Leopold admitted that Bobby was chosen "by pure accident." "He just happened along, and we got him," said Loeb.

THE PLAN IN ACTION

On May 21, the day of the kidnapping, Leopold and Loeb drove to a school in their neighborhood to look for a victim. They talked to Tommy,

Loeb's brother, and to a few other students. Then they saw Bobby Franks walking home. They knew Bobby because he lived in their neighborhood. He often played tennis at the court in Loeb's backyard. They pulled their car up next to Bobby and asked him to look at a tennis racquet they had in the back seat. When Bobby got in, they hit him over the head with a chisel wrapped in tape. Next they stuffed a rag down his throat. Bobby died very quickly.

Leopold and Loeb needed to wait until it was dark before they could dump Bobby's body. They drove around in the country outside Chicago and pulled over on the side of the road. They removed some of Bobby's clothing and threw it out the window. Next they went to a small restaurant and purchased hot dogs and root beer. They sat in the car eating their dinner with Bobby's body in the backseat.

When it was dark they returned to Chicago and went to Wolf Lake, where they had planned to leave Bobby. Leopold and Loeb stripped the body and poured acid over it.

This photograph, taken before his death in 1924, is a portrait of Bobby Franks standing outdoors in Chicago, Illinois. Like Leopold and Loeb, young Franks was wealthy, privileged, and smart. The photograph is now housed in the Chicago Historical Society.

They hoped that the acid would make the remains more difficult to identify. Finally, they stuffed his body into a ditch.

A photograph of the ransom note written by Leopold and Loeb and sent to Jacob Franks on May 21, 1924. The letter was mailed after the teenagers had murdered Bobby Franks and included instructions for throwing the ransom money off a train. Not long after Franks received the note, he learned that his son was dead. The image of the note and envelope was made in Chicago, Illinois, and is housed in the Chicago Historical Society.

After they got rid of Bobby's body they mailed the ransom note. Then they made their phone call to the Franks home. Returning to Loeb's house, they burned the rest of Bobby's clothes. They next went to Leopold's house, where they played cards and talked to Leopold's family. On the drive back to Loeb's house, they threw the chisel they had used to kill Bobby out the car window. They thought they had taken care of all the details and that they would never be caught. They were sure they had committed the perfect crime.

FINDING THE KILLERS

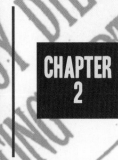

Robert E. Crowe was put in charge of the investigation of the murder of Bobby Franks. He was the state's attorney of Chicago and was in charge of prosecuting crimes in Chicago. When Crowe first heard about Bobby's murder, he told the *Evening Dispatch* newspaper that it was "one of the worst crimes in the history of the city. We must and will clear up this murder."

CHICAGO REACTS

There were about twelve newspapers in Chicago in the 1920s. In the days following Bobby's murder, every paper printed story after story about the murder. People were shocked by the murder of a child, and they wanted to read as much as possible about the case.

Newspaper readers had many theories about what had happened to Bobby Franks. Some newspapers offered as much as $10,000 for information about the case The papers got all kinds of tips, although none of them led anywhere. One lead was from a psychic in Kansas who said

Although 1920s Chicago was notorious for its overabundance of murders and other crimes, the Leopold and Loeb case shocked residents nonetheless. This photograph, taken in Chicago, Illinois, in 1924, shows crowds standing in front of the courthouse where the Bobby Franks murder trial was held. The photograph was taken by a *Chicago Daily News* photographer and is now housed in the Chicago Historical Society.

that two young men and a woman with red hair were involved. A few red-haired women in Bobby Franks's neighborhood were arrested because of this.

After a story about the ransom note being typed on a Corona typewriter appeared, the police got a tip about three young men carrying a Corona typewriter. When the police located the men, they found that they were typewriter repairmen. It seemed that every clue led to a dead end.

THE INVESTIGATION BEGINS

In the first few days after Bobby's body was found, the police did not have many solid leads. They decided to start their investigation at the school Bobby attended. Three teachers at the school were the first suspects. After they were questioned, all three were released.

The best clue the police had was the glasses that had been found near the body. Owners of eyeglass stores all over Chicago began trying to find out who had purchased the glasses.

The police looked for people who might have known about the area where Bobby's body was found. It was a popular place for bird-watching, and several people told them that Nathan Leopold often watched birds there. Leopold was an expert on birds and often taught bird-watching classes near Wolf Lake. Three days after Bobby's body was found, Leopold was brought in for questioning. He admitted that he often went to Wolf Lake. He also admitted that he wore glasses. However, the police did not suspect him and let him go.

While the police were working on their leads, journalists Mulroy and Goldstein were doing some investigating of their own. The day after Bobby's body was discovered, the two newspaper reporters happened to visit the University of Chicago. Goldstein had gone to college there and belonged to the same fraternity that Loeb belonged to.

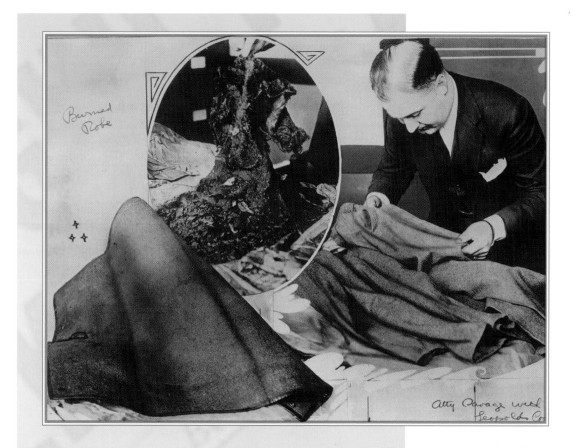

Taken on June 9, 1924, in Chicago, Illinois, this photographic montage shows three pieces of evidence used in Leopold and Loeb's trial. At right, assistant state's attorney Joseph Savage examines the coat and pants that Nathan Leopold wore when he killed Bobby Franks. The rug shown on the left is from the death car. **Inset:** The burnt remains of the auto robe (seat cover) that was used to cover Franks's body.

Loeb was at the fraternity that day, and he was very excited about the case. He suggested to Mulroy and Goldstein that they should try to find the drugstore where Mr. Franks was supposed to go to get more instructions for delivering the ransom. Loeb was still so sure that he wouldn't be caught that he was leading the reporters straight to an important clue! (Loeb had also bragged to friends about being a killer a few days after the murder.) When Loeb helped them locate the right drugstore, Mulroy and Goldstein called the police.

THE GLASSES LEAD TO A KILLER

The search for the owner of the glasses finally paid off. A worker at a Chicago eyeglass store spent more than thirty-six hours looking through the store's records. He traced the hinges of the frame and found that only three pairs of glasses with those hinges had been sold in Chicago. One of those three pairs had been sold to Nathan Leopold.

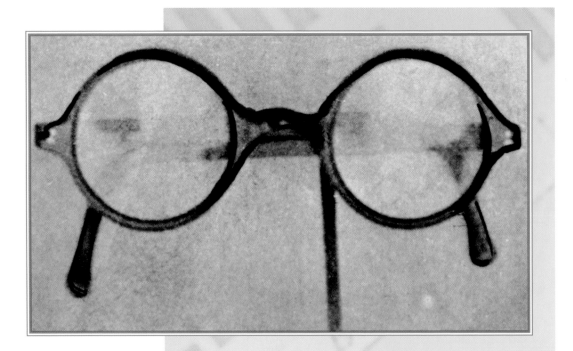

Seen by many as the piece of evidence that proved the killers' guilt, Nathan Leopold's eyeglasses fell out of his pocket while he "buried" Bobby Franks and were found when the body was discovered. Ironically, Leopold had stopped wearing glasses months before the murder, when the headaches for which they were prescribed subsided. He didn't even realize they had been in his breast pocket until he saw their photograph in a newspaper. This photograph of the spectacles was taken long after the trial, on July 30, 1957, in Chicago, Illinois.

Robert Crowe decided to have Leopold brought in again for questioning. Leopold admitted that he had often visited the area where the body had been found. He told investigators it was possible that he had dropped the glasses while bird watching. At first they believed him. When they asked him where he had been the day of the kidnapping, Leopold said he did not remember. This made the officials suspicious, and they decided to ask him more questions.

Leopold quickly changed his story and said that he and Loeb had gotten drunk the afternoon of the kidnapping. Later they had dinner and picked up two girls. The police asked him question after question about his story. They questioned him until 4:00 AM.

When Leopold told Crowe that he had been with Loeb on the day of the kidnapping, Loeb was brought in for questioning, too. He told a story similar to Leopold's. Crowe and the other lawyers thought the boys might be innocent. They were soon to get some evidence that would make them think otherwise.

THE REPORTERS STRIKE AGAIN

Once again Mulroy and Goldstein were on the trail of an important lead. They tried to trace the typewriter that had been used to type the ransom note. They knew Leopold had been brought in for questioning so they began to look for typewriters he might have used. They found some notes he had typed for school, but the type did not match the ransom note.

The reporters did not give up that easily. They talked to friends of Leopold's who remembered that Leopold had once used a portable typewriter to type their school notes. When the reporters found the notes that had been typed on the portable typewriter they realized the type was the same as on the ransom note. They took the two samples to an expert. He agreed that the ransom note and Leopold's study notes had been typed on the same typewriter.

Avon Public Library

This 1924 photograph shows Chicago state's attorney Robert Crowe *(left)* and investigators examining the manual Corona typewriter used by Nathan Leopold to type the ransom note sent to Jacob Franks. After the correct typewriter was discovered, Leopold's chauffeur tried to clear the young man's name but instead succeeded in underscoring his guilt. Soon after, Leopold and Loeb confessed to the kidnapping and murder of Bobby Franks.

Goldstein realized that this was very important information. He took it to Crowe immediately. Crowe began to think he might have caught the killer. He asked Leopold about the typewriter. Leopold said it did not belong to him. Crowe did not believe him and sent someone to Leopold's house to search for it. The portable typewriter was nowhere to be found. However, the Leopolds' housekeeper said she remembered seeing it.

A CONFESSION

Crowe thought he might be getting close to cracking the case. He wanted to check out other parts of Leopold and Loeb's story. He questioned the chauffeur who worked at Leopold's house. Leopold and Loeb had told the police that they had driven Leopold's car the day of Bobby's kidnapping. The chauffeur told Crowe a different story. Leopold's car had been in the garage all day.

Crowe began to question Leopold and Loeb again. Neither of the young men would confess to the crime. However, when Crowe told Loeb that Leopold's chauffeur had told him the car had been in the garage all day, Loeb grew pale and shaky. Loeb realized that he and his friend were trapped. It was all over. At almost 2:00 AM on Saturday, May 31, Loeb confessed.

Leopold still refused to talk. When Crowe began telling him details from Loeb's confession, Leopold realized that he, too, was trapped, so he confessed. Although some of the details in the two confessions were a little different, Leopold and Loeb agreed on most of the story. Neither of them would admit to killing Bobby, though. Each accused the other of being the one who had hit Bobby over the head.

PREPARING FOR TRIAL

News of the confessions traveled quickly. Reporters waited outside the rooms where Leopold and Loeb were being questioned. As soon as the reporters got the news, they called their offices. Newspapers began printing special editions with details about the confessions. Many thought that the young men should get the death penalty.

People all over Chicago were shocked by the news. They could not believe that smart young men like Leopold and Loeb could be killers. Leopold's and Loeb's families were just as shocked. They couldn't believe that the young men had committed such a terrible crime. They knew that they had to do all they could to prevent them from being executed. They had to get the boys a very good lawyer. That lawyer was Clarence Darrow.

DARROW TAKES THE CASE

Clarence Darrow had years of experience defending criminals. He was sixty-seven years old when he took the Leopold and Loeb case. He had tried many important and well-known cases.

Height	65.8	L. Foot	25.8	Col. of Eyes	Age,	19	Beard,	Ck Dk
Eng. H'ght	5.5 1/4	L. M. Fin.	11.9	On Dark	Apparent Age,		Hair,	Ck. Dk
Hd. Length	19.9	L. L. Fin.	9.4	Lt. Blue	Nativ. Illinois		Comp.	med
Hd. Width	13.9	L. Fore A.	47.0		Occu. Student		Weight,	137

Remarks Incident to Measurement

Build *need*

Teeth *Good*

Chin *Med. Rather sharp pt.*

Remarks

FPG   1   U   OI   8
      1   U   OO   15

Measured at Joliet, Illinois, State Penitentiary.   *Sept 12, 1924*

W. L. Petty

This 1924 image, now housed in the Chicago Historical Society, shows police photographs and physical records of Nathan Leopold. It was taken by a *Chicago Daily News* photographer. The measurements, assessments, and other information were taken by Joliet State Prison's W. L. Petty on September 12, 1924, when Leopold was admitted to the prison.

The Trial of Leopold and Loeb

Late at night, Loeb's uncle went to Darrow's house. According to Hal Higdon's book *Leopold and Loeb: The Crime of the Century*, he begged Darrow to take the case and help Leopold and Loeb avoid the death penalty. He told Darrow to "get them a life sentence instead . . . We'll pay anything, only for God's sake, don't let them hang."

Darrow knew he could not refuse. The Leopold and Loeb case would allow him to speak out against the death penalty. Darrow was

Clarence Darrow, defense attorney for the damned, sits with his clients Nathan Leopold *(left)* and Richard Loeb *(right)*, in front of an unidentified man. In his autobiography, *Life Plus Ninety-Nine Years*, Leopold wrote of Darrow: "Mr. Darrow was many things—philosopher, humanitarian, lawyer, defender of the rights of the underdog . . . To me, at least, Mr. Darrow's fundamental characteristic was his deep-seated, all-embracing kindliness. You couldn't look at the man without being struck almost instantly by this keynote of his character."

criticized for taking the case. Many people believed he had taken the case only to make money. Darrow knew he had taken the case for much more important reasons.

CROWE AND DARROW HIRE EXPERTS

After Leopold and Loeb confessed, Crowe knew he needed to find out if they were sane or not. If they were judged legally insane, they might be able to avoid getting the death penalty. Crowe did not want this to happen. He hired three doctors from Chicago who specialized in mental illness to examine the boys. Crowe hoped the doctors would prove that Leopold and Loeb knew exactly what they were doing when they brutally murdered Bobby Franks.

Clarence Darrow decided to hire some of his own doctors to examine Leopold and Loeb. He, too, wanted to find out if they were sane or insane. He hoped to show that they had psychological problems that led them to commit the crime. The doctors gave them physical and mental exams and talked to family members and other people who knew Leopold and Loeb.

Day after day the doctors examined Leopold and Loeb. The young men were questioned for hours about every part of their lives. They were given test after test and examination after examination. Leopold enjoyed the tests because he liked to talk about himself. The tests also gave

Lorraine Nathan testifies in the Leopold and Loeb trial in this 1924 photograph, taken by a photographer from the *Chicago Daily News*. Nathan broke off her casual relationship with Loeb because of his strange behavior. The photograph is housed in the Chicago Historical Society.

him a chance to show off how smart he was. Loeb was bored by the tests. He even fell asleep during sessions with the doctors. When the doctors were finished with all of their tests, they put together a 300-page report on the young men.

The experts hired by Crowe and Darrow learned many things about the lives of Leopold and Loeb. Loeb was very smart and read a lot. He liked reading books about crime. He went to college at an early age and tried hard to be like the older boys in his classes. He started drinking and talking a lot about girls so he could fit in. He worried so much about fitting in that he began to consider killing himself. He also began to think about committing a perfect crime. In his plan for the perfect crime, he wouldn't get caught, but the case would get a lot of publicity. Loeb admitted that murdering Bobby Franks was the perfect crime he had been thinking about for a long time.

Leopold was even smarter than Loeb. He graduated with honors from the University of Chicago when he was only eighteen years old. He started law school the fall before committing the crime. Leopold had studied fifteen languages and could speak five of them very well. Like Loeb, Leopold had a hard time fitting in with boys his own age. When he and Loeb met, Leopold knew he had found someone he fit in with. He and Loeb talked about Loeb's idea for a perfect crime, and Leopold was eager to help Loeb carry out his plan. Leopold liked and admired Loeb so much that he was willing to do anything Loeb asked him to do.

This 1924 *Chicago Daily News* photograph, now housed in the Chicago Historical Society, shows juvenile psychiatric expert Dr. William Healy testifying on behalf of the defense. Dr. Healy told the court, "To my mind the crime itself is the direct result of diseased motivation of Loeb's mental life. The planning and commission was only possible because he was abnormal mentally, with a pathological split personality." Leopold shook up the doctor by stating "Making up my mind whether or not to commit murder was practically the same as making up my mind whether or not I should eat pie for supper."

Leopold and Loeb were not very happy, and they had discussed killing each other, or killing themselves. Neither spent a lot of time thinking about what was right or wrong. In fact, when they talked to the doctors, they never said that they were sorry for Bobby or his family.

CHICAGO WAITS FOR THE TRIAL

Excitement about the trial began to build in Chicago. Day after day the many newspapers in Chicago were filled with stories about the case, including interviews with Leopold and Loeb in prison. The stories described what the young men wore, what they ate, what they did. The *Chicago Tribune* hired a man to study what the shapes of their faces, ears, and noses revealed about them. The *Chicago Herald-Examiner* found an astrologist to tell how their zodiac signs had made them murderers.

The papers also published stories about the tests that the doctors were giving Leopold and Loeb. They let the public participate by printing the tests in the paper. People wanted to see if they could do the tests as fast and as well as Leopold. The *Chicago Tribune* even tried to get the famous psychiatrist Sigmund Freud to come to Chicago. The paper offered him $25,000 to study Leopold and Loeb. Freud was not very healthy and could not make the trip from Europe.

Another thing Chicago residents got to read before the trial was the 300-page report prepared by the doctors Darrow hired. It was stolen from Darrow's office and printed in newspapers. Some people suggested that Darrow gave it to reporters so that people could read it before it appeared in court. The report made people feel sorry for Leopold and Loeb. It made the pair seem like ordinary—but lonely—boys.

People in cities all over the country read stories about Leopold and Loeb. A man from Milwaukee offered to be put to death in place of either Leopold or Loeb. He asked only that his family be paid $1 million. He told the *Chicago Daily News*, "I am ready to be hung any time the law is ready to call on me, as there is no glory in life ahead of me."

Leopold and Loeb spent their first few weeks in jail being interviewed by reporters and doctors. Neither seemed too worried about the upcoming trial. In fact, Leopold looked forward to it. He was eager to see Clarence Darrow in action. Leopold was pretty sure he and Loeb would get the death penalty. In a later interview, he admitted that he hoped to plead guilty and hang in order to decrease the suffering that all parties would endure.

Loeb did not feel much of anything at all. According to Hal Higdon in his book *Leopold and Loeb: The Crime of the Century*, Loeb told a reporter, "I know I should feel sorry I killed that young man and all that, but I just don't feel it. I didn't have much feeling about this from the first. That's why I could do it. There was nothing inside of me to stop me. Of course, I'm sorry about my family, but not as much as I ought to be."

THE PROSECUTION BEGINS ITS CASE

The trial that everyone had been waiting for finally began Monday, July 21, 1924. However, it turned out not to be the trial most people expected. Dressed neatly, Leopold and Loeb waited quietly with their lawyers in the courtroom. Judge John R. Caverly took his place in front of the room. Caverly was sixty-three years old and had been a judge for fourteen years.

Leopold and Loeb's famous lawyer, Clarence Darrow, was the first to speak. Everyone waited to hear what he would say. Darrow admitted that everyone knew Leopold and Loeb should be locked up. It was clear that they were guilty. In fact, it was so clear that they were guilty that he had decided to change their plea to guilty.

This shocked everyone in the room, including Darrow's opponent Crowe. Everyone had expected a long trial ending with a jury deciding whether Leopold and Loeb were guilty. The jury would then determine whether the young men should get the death penalty. Darrow's

Judge John R. Caverly, chief justice of the Circuit Court of Cook County (Illinois), was known for taking an interest in young people; he had worked to establish a juvenile court in Chicago. Clarence Darrow counted on Caverly's kindness when he decided Leopold and Loeb should plead guilty to the murder of Bobby Franks. He knew Caverly would never execute the boys. Caverly is shown standing behind a courtroom desk in this photograph, taken by the *Chicago Daily News* and housed in the Chicago Historical Society.

plea of guilty for the two young men changed everything. That was just what Darrow was hoping.

DARROW'S PLAN

Darrow had a good reason for changing to a guilty plea. It would mean that Judge Caverly, not a jury, would decide on Leopold and Loeb's punishment. Darrow did not think he had any chance of getting a fair trial by a jury. Many stories had been written in the newspaper about the case. People were sure they already knew who had done it. Most people were also eager to see the young men get the death penalty for their brutal crime.

Darrow thought he might be able to convince Judge Caverly to give Leopold and Loeb life in prison instead of the death penalty. He knew that the judge would have to think hard about the decision. Darrow thought it would be easier for a jury to give the young men the death penalty. After all, there are twelve people on a jury, and they would all share the burden of their decision. On the other hand, if the judge sentenced the young men to death he would have no one to blame but himself.

Darrow had two points he hoped he could use to convince the judge that Leopold and Loeb should not get the death penalty. One was the young age of both men. The other was the psychological state of each. Darrow did not think they were insane, and he did not want them to avoid punishment by saying they were. He did want to show, however, that they were not responsible for their actions. He wanted to prove that they had committed their crime because of their "mental problems."

In some court cases before this one, lawyers had proven that their clients were insane. In those cases, their clients had avoided the death penalty because it was determined that they were not of sound mind

In this 1924 photograph, taken in the courtroom of the Leopold and Loeb trial, Clarence Darrow makes an argument to Judge Caverly that his case depends on the testimony of psychiatric experts. Caverly's allowance of this testimony proved to be crucial to keeping the teenagers from receiving the death sentence. The doctors convinced the judge that Leopold and Loeb's mental states strongly influenced their murderous actions.

when they committed the crimes. This would be the first time that a lawyer used evidence of mental problems to avoid the death penalty without claiming insanity.

Crowe quickly got over his shock at the change in plea. He had gathered plenty of evidence against Leopold and Loeb, and he would present it anyway. Leopold and Loeb had committed a terrible crime, and he planned to prove it. He told the *Chicago Tribune* that he would show "not only that these boys are guilty, but that they are absolutely sane and should be hanged."

Judge Caverly agreed to begin the trial—now technically a hearing, since a guilty plea had been entered—earlier than planned. It would start in two days. Although it would not be the trial everyone expected, it would surely be interesting.

OPENING STATEMENTS

On Wednesday, July 23, 1924, Leopold and Loeb sat in a courtroom once again. They smoked cigarettes and talked to reporters while they waited for the trial to begin. The room was packed. It could hold 300 people, and 200 of them were newspaper reporters and photographers. Each had to apply for a ticket to get in. Not everyone was able to get a ticket—even if they had traveled hundreds of miles to get to Chicago. There were seventy seats left over for the public, and people fought each other to get in. Everyone wanted to see the killers and find out what would happen to them.

Crowe was the first to speak. He told everyone that he would prove that Leopold and Loeb had killed Bobby Franks. When he had finished presenting his evidence, he planned to "demand the death penalty for both of these cold-blooded, cruel, and vicious murderers."

Darrow spoke next and agreed that everyone already knew Leopold and Loeb had killed Bobby. But Darrow was prepared to show that hanging Leopold and Loeb for their crime would not "bring back [Bobby] Franks or add to the peace and security of this community."

CROWE PRESENTS HIS CASE

Crowe and his four assistants began to present their evidence about every part of the case. Even though Leopold and Loeb had already

Posing for photographers, Richard Loeb sits inside the car he and Nathan Leopold used on the day they murdered Bobby Franks. Standing beside him is state's attorney Robert Crowe. Leopold and Loeb both agreed to pose for pictures, but curiously they refused to be photographed in the car together. This image was taken on June 3, 1924, in Chicago, Illinois.

confessed and pleaded guilty, Crowe wanted to make sure the details were known. He wanted to show that the young men had planned every step of the crime so they would not get caught. Crowe also wanted to show that the crime was very cruel and that Leopold and Loeb were not sorry they had done it. He hoped all these things would convince the judge to give them the death penalty.

Crowe and his team called numerous witnesses. The team questioned people who had sold things to Leopold and Loeb that they used in the crime. They questioned Bobby Franks's parents and the people who had found Bobby's body.

The first day, fifteen people came to the stand to testify for the prosecution. Darrow chose only to cross-examine, or question, one of Crowe's witnesses. He knew that if he questioned the witnesses it would only make their testimony more powerful. It would make the judge remember how horrible the crime had been.

It took Crowe one week to present all his witnesses. He finished on Wednesday, July 30. He had called eighty-one witnesses, and he had proven what he had set out to prove: Leopold and Loeb had murdered Bobby Franks.

Before the murder of Bobby Franks, no one who knew Leopold and Loeb thought they were mentally abnormal. Darrow's defense depended on people realizing that they were. He needed his experts to show that there were many things wrong with Leopold and Loeb. They had to describe how strange and immature the boys were.

The day after Crowe finished presenting the prosecution's side of the case, Darrow was ready to begin. His first witness was Dr. William White. White was one of the doctors that Darrow had hired to examine Leopold and Loeb. Dr. White told the judge that he didn't think Leopold would have kidnapped or killed Bobby alone. He didn't think that Loeb would have gone that far on his own either. He believed the crime was committed because of the combination of Leopold and Loeb.

The next expert, Dr. William Healy, believed that Loeb was "abnormal mentally" and that is why the crime was committed. The third expert agreed, telling the court that Loeb had confessed that he had "struck the blow" that killed Bobby. A few of Leopold and Loeb's

Dr. Harold Hulbert testifies on the stand in this photograph, taken by the *Chicago Daily News* during the trial in 1924. The photograph is now part of a Chicago Historical Society collection. Hulbert worked with Dr. Carl Bowman to study every detail of Leopold and Loeb's lives and compile the findings into a 300-page report that was widely published in the press. In his marathon sessions with the doctors, Loeb was bored, but Leopold took great joy in talking about himself.

friends and classmates testified next. They talked about Leopold and Loeb's sometimes strange behavior.

Dr. Harold Hulbert was the next expert to testify. He was one of the doctors who had written the long report about Leopold and Loeb that was published before the trial. He told the judge that both young men were very smart but also very immature. He thought they acted more like they were seven or eight years old. He agreed with Dr. White that each needed the other to commit the crime and that neither would have done it on his own. He and the other experts agreed that the young men knew that kidnapping and killing Bobby Franks was against the law. They wouldn't have done it if they thought they would be caught.

CROWE FINISHES HIS CASE

When Darrow was finished with his witnesses, Crowe had a few of his witnesses come back to testify again. Then Crowe called one of his expert doctors, Dr. Hugh Patrick. Dr. Patrick didn't believe that Leopold and Loeb were mentally abnormal and told the judge, "Unless we assume that every man who commits a deliberate, cold-blooded, planned murder must, by that fact, be mentally diseased, there is no evidence of mental disease." Crowe's next expert, Dr. Archibald Church, agreed with Dr. Patrick.

On August 19, Crowe finished presenting his evidence and witnesses. It was time for closing arguments. In their closing arguments, Crowe and his assistants asked Judge Caverly to do to Leopold and Loeb what they had done to Bobby. Joseph Savage, one of Crowe's assistants, told the courtroom, "This is the coldest-blooded murder that the civilized world ever saw . . . No one would strike a dog the way these murderers beat the life out of poor little Bobby Franks with a cold chisel." Savage told the judge that he had to give Leopold and Loeb the death penalty. If he didn't, how would any jury in Chicago be

The prosecutor Joseph Savage urges Judge Caverly to give Leopold and Loeb a death sentence in this 1924 image, taken in court by a *Chicago Daily News* photographer. The photograph is now housed in the Chicago Historical Society. Savage's words to the judge were passionate: "This is the coldest-blooded murder that the civilized world ever saw."

able to give the death penalty to anyone else? Crowe and his assistants spoke so harshly that many people in the courtroom cried. Even Leopold was shaken, perhaps for the first time in the whole trial.

DARROW'S TURN TO SPEAK

Finally, the moment many had been waiting for had arrived. It was almost time for the legendary Darrow to speak. When people heard the news that Darrow was going to begin his closing statements, hundreds tried to get into the courtroom. Extra police had to be called in to help manage the crowd. The horde was so noisy that Darrow could not be heard inside the courtroom. He had to wait to speak until the police finally moved everyone out of the building.

Darrow and everyone else in the courtroom knew that the success of his whole case depended on whether he could use his closing argument to convince Judge Caverly not to put Leopold and Loeb to death. If he failed, his clients would lose their lives.

Darrow began his speech by talking about how young Leopold and Loeb were. They were too young to vote (in 1924 the legal voting age was twenty-one) and too young to get married without their parents' permission. Darrow thought they were too young to be put to death. He reminded Judge Caverly that the Chicago municipal court had never imposed the death penalty to anyone under twenty-one. Darrow didn't think Caverly should be the first to do that.

Darrow admitted that Leopold and Loeb committed their crime for no good reason. It was "a senseless, useless, purposeless, motiveless act of two boys." Crowe had tried to argue that all their planning showed that they were sane. Darrow argued that instead it showed just how crazy they were. No one could "believe that one of these acts was the act of men with brains that were not diseased. There is no other explanation for it." The young men had kidnapped Bobby from a street in their own neighborhood where everyone knew them. They had left Bobby's body in the car when they went to buy dinner. Afterward, they talked about the crime with friends, reporters, and police. "There is not a sane thing in all of this from beginning to end," said Darrow.

Now it was time for Darrow to talk about the death penalty. He knew that many people wanted Leopold and Loeb to get the death penalty. However, Darrow wanted to convince the judge that the death penalty was no better than an "eye for an eye." He asked Judge Caverly

This 1924 photograph, taken by the *Chicago Daily News*, and now belonging to the Chicago Historical Society, shows Clarence Darrow speaking with Judge Caverly in the Chicago courtroom where Leopold and Loeb's trial was held. "I am pleading for life, understanding, charity, kindness, and the infinite mercy that considers all," he told the court.

to think about whether the world would be a better place if Leopold and Loeb were executed. Darrow said he didn't think it would be, because "hatred only causes hatred." He argued that "if there is any way to kill evil and hatred and all that goes with it, it is not through evil and hatred and cruelty, it is through charity and love and understanding."

Darrow did not just want to save Leopold and Loeb from the death penalty. He hoped that his speech would lead to the death penalty being abolished: "[My] greatest reward and my greatest hope will be that I have done something for the tens of thousands of other boys" who might find themselves in the same position as Leopold and Loeb. Darrow wanted to "do something to help human understanding [and] to overcome hate with love."

After three days of speaking, Darrow was finally done. Many people in the courtroom were crying when he finished, including Judge Caverly. Everyone agreed that his speech was brilliant. Many lawyers think it was the best speech he ever gave. It was simply worded and it made sense. In Gilbert Geis and Leigh B. Bienen's *Crimes of the Century*, Alan Dershowitz, a well-known contemporary lawyer, said Darrow "made it easy for the listener to agree with him."

THE JUDGE MAKES A DECISION

The trial was almost over. Before Judge Caverly could make his decision, Crowe had one last chance to speak. A newspaper story in the *Chicago Daily News* described Crowe's closing statements: "He spoke in a frenzy. He shouted and stamped and waved his arms . . . his eyes blazing and his voice screaming anger." He attacked Leopold and Loeb and Clarence Darrow. He made fun of Darrow's experts and their reports. He said the experts had been paid well to testify and shouldn't be trusted. Crowe reminded the judge that it was his job to make sure that laws were followed. People like Leopold and Loeb who don't follow the law should be punished. Crowe told the judge that Leopold and Loeb shouldn't get sympathy from anyone. They were "a couple of rattle-snakes, flushed with venom, and ready to strike."

Crowe spoke for nearly three days. On the third day of his speech his voice began to give out, and he could barely finish. Then the trial was over. All that remained was a decision from the judge. Judge Caverly said he would make his decision in about ten days.

Avon Public Library

THE JUDGE'S DECISION

On Wednesday, September 10, 1924, Leopold and Loeb entered the courtroom to find out what their fate would be. Before the judge gave them his decision he asked the young men if they had anything to say. Both said no, so Judge Caverly began to speak.

There was no question that Leopold and Loeb were guilty. There was plenty of evidence and they had confessed. It was clear to the judge that Leopold and Loeb weren't insane, although they were abnormal. There was no specific law that could help him decide what to do with the boys. However, the judge agreed with Darrow that they were just too young to get the death penalty. He decided not to "impose the sentence of death on persons who are not of full age." There had been only two other times in the state of Illinois where people under eighteen were put to death. Judge Caverly did not want to add to that number.

The judge decided that Leopold and Loeb should be sentenced to life in prison for murdering Bobby Franks. To each one's sentence he added ninety-nine years for the kidnapping. Judge Caverly also strongly suggested that neither should ever be let out of prison on parole.

REACTION TO THE DECISION

Clarence Darrow was very happy with the judge's decision. He was glad that he had saved his clients from being put to death. He hoped the verdict would help end the death penalty for good.

Loeb's father spoke for both families. In his statement, he said they were happy the young men would not be put to death. There was not much else that was good about the situation, though. "What is there in the future but grief, sorrow, darkness, and despair?" he asked.

Bobby Franks's parents were satisfied with the young men being sent to prison. Mr. Franks told reporters that he and his wife "never believed [Leopold and Loeb] should be hanged."

Clarence Darrow stands between Nathan Leopold *(left)* and Richard Loeb as they hear Judge Caverly's decision, in this photograph, taken September 10, 1924, in a Chicago courtroom. Before giving the murderers their sentence, Caverly said, "Life imprisonment, at the moment, strikes the public imagination as forcibly as would death by hanging, but to the offenders, particularly of the type they are, the prolonged suffering of years of confinement may well be the severest form of retribution and expiation."

Many people in Chicago were not pleased by the decision. They thought this might make it easier for murderers to be spared the death penalty in the future. Some thought that Leopold and Loeb had gotten special treatment because their families were rich. Most people hoped that Leopold and Loeb would never be released from prison.

LIFE IN PRISON

The night after they were sentenced, Leopold and Loeb were taken to the state prison in Joliet, Illinois. On the way to the prison the young

This 1924 news photograph shows Richard Loeb *(left)* and Nathan Leopold being escorted into Joliet State Prison in Chicago. In keeping with their privileged upbringings, the boys were permitted catered food, alcohol (illegal during that time because of Prohibition), and cigarettes while in jail before their trial. Their stay at Joliet was not quite so comfortable.

men were guarded well to prevent them from escaping—and from being attacked. Many people were not happy with the judge's decision, and police were worried that Leopold and Loeb would be harmed.

During their first year in prison both boys were sick. Sometimes they were sent to solitary confinement. There they were locked to the bars of the cell with only a concrete bench to sleep on. They had only bread and water to eat, and they had to use a bucket instead of a toilet.

In 1931, Leopold and Loeb started a school for other prisoners. They taught many subjects and organized a library for prisoners to use. Early in 1936, Loeb was attacked in the bathroom of the prison school. Another prisoner slashed him repeatedly with a razor, and Loeb died from his wounds. Leopold got to sit with him before he died and was very upset. He had lost his best friend.

Now Leopold was alone in prison for what he thought would be the rest of his life. He tried to keep busy. He studied twelve more languages, took college courses by mail, and learned how to use an x-ray machine. He worked in the prison library and even taught Sunday school.

Leopold's first chance at getting parole came in 1953. Officials met to decide if Leopold should be released from prison. Most felt that he should not be freed. At the meeting they asked Leopold why he had committed his crime. He said, "I couldn't give a motive which makes sense to me. [It was] a very bizarre act. I don't know why I did it. I'm a different man now." The officials didn't agree and voted to keep him in prison.

A NEW LIFE

Now Leopold would have to wait twelve more years for his next chance at parole. He didn't want to wait that long, so in 1957, he asked the governor of Illinois to set him free. Another meeting was held to decide if he should be released. This time Leopold tried harder to explain why he had committed his crime. He said that he had admired Loeb and wanted to prove that he could do what Loeb asked of him. In his autobiography, *Life Plus Ninety-Nine Years,* he would explain himself further: "I committed my crime because I admired Loeb extravagantly, because I didn't want to be a quitter, and because I wanted to show that I had the nerve to do what he insisted on doing . . . I was completely carried away by my admiration for Loeb."

After serving only thirty-three years of his life sentence, Nathan Leopold was released from Joliet State Prison. In this photograph, taken on March 13, 1958, by Steve Marino, Leopold speaks with reporters about his plans for the future. Thirteen years later, after moving to Puerto Rico, marrying, teaching, and writing, Nathan Leopold would die at the age of sixty-six.

Leopold admitted that these were not very good reasons for killing Bobby Franks. Several people testified for and against Leopold getting out of prison. This time the outcome was different. Leopold was released from prison on March 13, 1958. He had been behind bars for over thirty-three years.

The day after Leopold was released he flew to Puerto Rico. He got a job at a hospital and worked there for two years. He also went back to college, taught classes at the University of Puerto Rico, did medical research, and wrote an autobiography. Leopold made the most of his freedom. 1n 1961, he married Trudi Feldman Garcia de Quereda, a former social worker, and lived the rest of his life in Puerto Rico. He died on August 30, 1971, at age sixty-six, of heart problems.

THE CRIME OF THE CENTURY

The Leopold and Loeb case was called the Crime of the Century in 1924, when the century was still very young. Cases like the Scopes Trial, about the teaching of evolution, and the O. J. Simpson murder trial came along later and were also called the Crime of the Century. It is a matter of opinion which crime was the crime of the century. All of them caught the attention of the country. All of them made people focus on the legal system.

The Leopold and Loeb case called attention to psychological issues and the role they played in the legal system. The case showed that with a good defense it could be proven that a person was led to commit a crime by his or her mental disturbances. This did not necessarily mean that the person was legally insane.

The case also brought attention to lawyers using expert witnesses, like the doctors called to the stand by both Crowe and Darrow. In 1924, this was still a new practice. Many people thought that experts were paid to say whatever they were told. This is still an issue that people debate in our legal system.

THE DEATH PENALTY

The death penalty had been used in the United States—even for children—since the first colonies were formed. In the early days of the country, people could be put to death for breaking all kinds of laws, including murder, witchcraft, and even swearing.

Did the Leopold and Loeb case do anything to change the death penalty in America? Even though Darrow (and many others) continued to speak out against it, it is still in use in the United States today. It does not appear that the case of Leopold and Loeb did anything to change its use in the United States. Since the first execution of a child under eighteen in 1642 (sixteen-year-old Thomas Graungery), there have been more than 350 executions of children in the United States. As of February 2001, only thirteen states do not have the death penalty. The rest have a death penalty with a minimum age of sixteen, seventeen, or eighteen.

When Judge Caverly decided not to execute Leopold and Loeb, his main reason was their ages. Today Leopold and Loeb would not be considered minors. It is unlikely that their ages would have kept them from getting the death penalty.

It is no surprise that the crime Leopold and Loeb committed in 1924 is still remembered today. Two smart, wealthy young men decided to murder a boy. Why? Leopold and Loeb never could answer that question, and we still don't have a good answer today. The case—and the trial—will continue to fascinate us.

GLOSSARY

abolish   To get rid of completely.

astrologer   Person who studies how positions of the stars and planets affect human behavior.

chauffeur   Someone paid to drive a car.

chisel   A sharp metal tool with a blade used to dig into wood, metal, or stone.

confess   To admit to a crime.

contemporary   Present-day.

cross-examine   To question a witness already examined by the other side.

death penalty   A sentence of punishment by death.

defense   The lawyer or team of lawyers representing the accused.

gangster   A member of a group of criminals.

horde   A large group or crowd.

immature   Young and inexperienced.

juveniles   Children or young people.

lead   A clue that helps solve a case.

legendary   Famous.

outlawed   Made illegal.

parole   Early release from prison.

plea   The official answer to a charge in court.

prosecuting   Leading a legal action against someone accused of a crime.

psychiatrist   A doctor who studies the mind and behavior.

psychic   A person who claims to see or sense people or events that are not actually present.

ransom   Money paid in exchange for someone who has been kidnapped.

remains   A dead body.

scandal   An event that shocks or offends people.

testimony   Official statements made by witnesses in court.

zodiac   The star sign someone is born under, such as Aries or Taurus.

FOR MORE INFORMATION

The American Bar Association Museum of Law
750 North Lake Shore Drive
Chicago, IL 60611-3152
(312) 988-6222

Amnesty International
322 Eighth Avenue
New York, NY 10001
(212) 807-8400
Web site: http://www.aiusa.org

Chicago Historical Society
Clark Street at North Avenue
Chicago, IL 60614-6071
(312) 642-4600
Web site: http://www.chicagohs.org

WEB SITES

Due to the changing nature of Internet links, the Rosen Publishing Group, Inc., has developed an online list of Web sites related to the subject of this book. This site is updated regularly. Please use this link to access the list:

http://www.rosenlinks.com/gttc/trll

FOR FURTHER READING

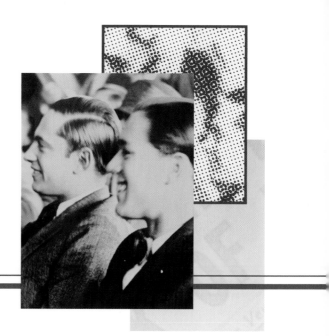

Drieman, John E. *Clarence Darrow*. New York: Chelsea House
Publishers, 1992.

Emert, Phyllis Raybin. *Top Lawyers and Their Famous Cases*.
Minneapolis: The Oliver Press, Inc., 1996.

Gottfried, Ted. *Capital Punishment: The Death Penalty Debate*.
Springfield, NJ: Enslow Publishers, Inc., 1997.

Kraft, Betsy Harvey. *Sensational Trials of the 20th Century*. New York:
Scholastic Press, 1998.

Stewart, Gail B. *The Death Penalty*. San Diego, CA: Greenhaven
Press, Inc., 1998.

BIBLIOGRAPHY

Busch, Francis X. *Prisoners at the Bar: An Account of the Trials of the William Haywood Case, the Sacco-Vanzetti Case, the Loeb-Leopold Case, and the Bruno Hauptmann Case.* Freeport, NY: Books for Libraries Press, 1970.

Clarence Darrow's Sentencing Speech: *State of Illinois v. Leopold and Loeb.* Minnetonka, MN: Professional Education Group, 1988.

Fass, Paula S. "Making and Remaking an Event: The Leopold and Loeb Case in American Culture." *Journal of American History,* Vol. 80, No. 3 (December 1993), pp. 919–951.

Geis, Gilbert, and Leigh B. Bienen. *Crimes of the Century: From Leopold and Loeb to O.J. Simpson.* Boston: Northeastern University Press, 1998.

Higdon, Hal. *Leopold and Loeb: The Crime of the Century.* Urbana, IL: University of Chicago Press, 1999.

Mackey, Philip English, ed. *Voices Against Death: American Opposition to Capital Punishment 1787–1975.* New York: Burt Franklin & Co., Inc., 1976.

Newman, Scott A. "Jazz Age Chicago: The Leopold and Loeb Case." 1997. Retrieved June 3, 2002 (http://www.suba.com/~scottn/explore/scrapbks/leo_loeb/leo_loeb.htm).

Shattuck, Roger. "When Evil Is Cool." *Atlantic Monthly*. January 1999. Retrieved June 22, 2002 (http://www.theatlantic.com/issues/99jan/evil.htm).

Streib, Victor L. "The Juvenile Death Penalty Today: Death Sentences and Executions for Juvenile Crimes, January 1, 1973–December 31, 2001." Ohio Northern University. 2002. Retrieved June 24, 2002 (http://www.law.onu.edu/faculty/streib/juvdeath.htm).

Szumski, Bonnie, Lynn Hall, and Susan Bursell, eds. *The Death Penalty: Opposing Viewpoints.* Saint Paul, MN: Greenhaven Press, 1986.

Weinberg, Arthur, ed. *Attorney for the Damned: Clarence Darrow in the Courtroom.* Chicago: University of Chicago Press, 1989.

PRIMARY SOURCE IMAGE LIST

Cover and page 1: Photograph of Nathan Leopold Jr. and Richard Loeb in jail, taken on June 4, 1924, in Chicago, Illinois.

Page 4: Photograph of Nathan Leopold and Richard Loeb in court, taken in 1924 in Chicago, Illinois.

Page 8: Photograph of police officers finding the body of Bobby Franks, taken on May 23, 1924, outside of Chicago, Illinois.

Page 9: Photograph of Jacob Franks, taken by a *Chicago Daily News* photographer in 1924. Housed in the Chicago Historical Society.

Page 10: Photograph of Richard Loeb and Nathan Leopold, taken on July 21, 1924, in Chicago, Illinois.

Page 12: Photographic portrait of James Mulroy and Alvin Goldstein, taken by a *Chicago Daily News* photographer in 1924 in Chicago, Illinois. Housed in the Chicago Historical Society.

Page 13: Photographic portrait of Bobby Franks, taken in Chicago, Illinois, in 1924. Housed in the Chicago Historical Society.

Page 14: Photograph of May 21, 1924, ransom letter and envelope sent to Jacob Franks. Image taken in Chicago, Illinois, in 1924 and housed in the Chicago Historical Society.

Page 17: Photograph of crowds outside the courthouse during the Leopold and Loeb trial. Taken in 1924 by a photographer for the *Chicago Daily News*. Housed in the Chicago Historical Society.

Page 19: Photographs of car rug, robe, and Joseph Savage inspecting clothing, taken June 9, 1924, in Chicago, Illinois.

Page 20: Photograph of Nathan Leopold's eyeglasses, taken on July 30, 1957, in Chicago, Illinois.

Page 22: Photograph of Robert Crowe with investigators and portable typewriter, taken in 1924 in Chicago, Illinois.

Page 25: Photograph of police mug shots and Joliet State Prison physical records of Nathan Leopold Jr., taken in 1924. Housed in the Chicago Historical Society.

Page 26: Photograph of Nathan Leopold Jr., Clarence Darrow, and Richard Loeb with a court officer. Taken in 1924, in Chicago, Illinois.

Page 27: Photograph of Lorraine Nathan in a courtroom in Chicago, Illinois. Taken by a *Chicago Daily News* photographer in 1924. Housed in the Chicago Historical Society.

Page 29: Photograph of Dr. William Healy in a courtroom in Chicago, Illinois. Taken by a *Chicago Daily News* photographer in 1924. Housed in the Chicago Historical Society.

Page 33: Photograph of Judge John R. Caverly in a courtroom in Chicago, Illinois. Taken by a *Chicago Daily News* photographer in 1924. Housed in the Chicago Historical Society.

Page 35: Photograph of Clarence Darrow in a Chicago, Illinois, courtroom. Taken in 1924.

Page 37: Photograph of Richard Loeb and Robert Crowe with car. Taken on June 3, 1924, in Chicago, Illinois.

Page 40: Photograph of Dr. Harold Hulbert on the stand. Taken by a *Chicago Daily News* photographer in 1924. Housed in the Chicago Historical Society.

Page 42: Photograph of Joseph Savage in court. Taken in Chicago, Illinois, by a *Chicago Daily News* photographer in 1924. Housed in the Chicago Historical Society.

Page 44: Photograph of Clarence Darrow with Judge Caverly. Taken by a *Chicago Daily News* photographer in 1924. Housed in the Chicago Historical Society.

Page 47: Photograph of Nathan Leopold, Clarence Darrow, and Richard Loeb. Taken in Chicago, Illinois, on September 10, 1924.

Page 48: Photograph of Richard Loeb and Nathan Leopold in prison. Taken in the summer of 1924 in Chicago, Illinois.

Page 50: Photograph of Nathan Leopold speaking to the press. Taken on March 13, 1958, in Joliet, Illinois.

INDEX

ABOUT THE AUTHOR

Simone Payment has a degree in psychology from Cornell University and a master's degree in elementary education from Wheelock College. She is also the author of a biography of the Negro league baseball star Buck Leonard, a biography of the French explorer La Salle, and books about travel careers and Navy SEALs.

ACKNOWLEDGMENTS

The author would like to thank Howard Cooper, Lori Cooper, Marina Lang, and Jennifer Marcus for their valuable insights, suggestions, and continued support.

CREDITS

Cover, pp. 1, 4, 8, 10, 19, 20, 22, 25, 26, 37, 47, 48, 51 © Bettmann/Corbis; pp. 9, 12, 13, 14, 17, 27, 29, 33, 35, 40, 42, 44 *Chicago Daily News* negatives collection, Chicago Historical Society.

Series Design: Les Kanturek; **Editor:** Christine Poolos